Picking the Right Natural Hair Products for your Curly, Kinky Hair

Find the BEST Ingredients, Save Time and Save Money

By Darice Rene

http://www.DariceRene.com

all other aspects of doing business in the US, Canada, or any other jurisdiction is the sole responsibility of the purchaser or reader.

Neither the author nor the publisher assumes any responsibility or liability whatsoever on the behalf of the purchaser or reader of these materials.

Any perceived slight of any individual or organization is purely unintentional.

Your Free Gift

I'm excited that you've decided to read *Picking the Right Natural Hair Products for your Curly, Kinky Hair*. As a way of saying thank you, I'd like to offer you a free gift.

Natural hair can certainly be a mystery. I've created some free tools for you to be certain that you're moving in the right direction with your hair. Simply sign up for regular updates at www.naturalhairindy.com for your gifts.

Dedication

To Brianna and Caleb, my life's greatest joy. You make me proud every day.

And to my husband, Charlie, for applying just the right amount of pressure. I thank you.

Table of Contents

Introduction

Hello. My name is Darice Rene and I've suffered some setbacks on my journey to natural hair.

I've done the big chop twice. The first time I had my hair stylist cut off all of my permed hair, it was to feel liberated. I had reached a milestone at work and was doing very well in Corporate America. I'd recently earned my Master's degree and it was the year I turned 30 so I kind of lost my mind – in a good way. Years of chemical relaxers had made my hair so fine and weak that you could merely walk past me and a few hair strands would fall to the floor. I was also tired of sitting in beauty shops for hours and missing out on activities like swimming and working out because of my hair.

Everything was going well. I didn't know very much about my hair so I wore it in a puff mostly but it was stronger and healthier so I didn't mind.

My hair care standards were pretty low at that time. I was laid off work from the finance industry, however, which changed everything. I made a decision to relax my hair. I felt like my natural hair might intimidate would-be employers so in order to make them more comfortable with how I looked, despite my credentials, I gave in to the fear of not fitting in to my new surroundings.

The last relaxer I ever had was purchased from a Korean-owned beauty supply store. I'd been perming my hair off and on for years so I should have known something was wrong when I mixed the ingredients and the product was crunchy. Tired from work and figuring it would all work out somehow, I applied the relaxer and later watched chunks of my hair fall down the drain of my sink. It was a bad perm. The next morning I grabbed some leftover weave from my closet and drove to my first cousin, a licensed stylist. I could not have been more disgusted with myself because everything about that scenario was wrong. I'd put

4

chemicals in my hair to be accepted by others and this was the result. Within a week, I found a Great Clips salon near my house and had all my hair cut off a second time.

My buzz cut caused me some serious issues with my confidence. Regardless of what I had achieved in my life, I was still doubtful about my looks with this tiny Afro. I threw my energy into learning more about my hair and how to achieve certain looks. One day I bought a leather journal at TJ Maxx and begin to document everything. I kept track of products, styles that looked good on me, techniques to twist or roll or braid my hair and I paid attention to product ingredients. Within a year, I was transformed. I felt more confident, I felt more beautiful and I was even more poised. Although I would still don a wig from time to time, it was mostly to put my hair away in a protective style or to hide the fact that I hadn't felt like grooming it that day. I was in a great place, finally.

That place led me to seek kinship from other women with natural hair. I wanted to connect, share stories and learn about their experiences. I reached out to see if there were others like me and in the midst of that simple request, I have been able to build a community in my city. Our Meetup group boasts 800 members today and I've been able to lead workshops and organize over 30 events in under 3 years. I've also authored a blog to share what I know, with over 200 articles written about this passion. My interest and admiration for natural hair has resulted in working to help other women learn how to embrace their individual natural beauty. This book is a part of that work.

My Natural Hair Philosophy

I believe that a successful natural hair journey requires that women know their hair. And being successful is defined as being happy with how you look with natural hair. I don't believe that women should follow advice from everyone that they find until they have qualified the source. I also believe that hair care is important.

At the end of the day, everything that a woman does with her natural hair is to represent her own individual beauty.

What does being natural mean to me? It means that you are an individual. It means that you have embraced the new standard of beauty. A standard that is not defined by anyone but yourself. It also means freedom. By that, I mean that you are free to choose to do to your hair and to represent yourself in your highest ability as you see fit. It is also personal confidence. It means that a woman has decided who she is and needs no permissions for it.

Purpose of the book

This book is meant to help women with kinky and curly hair save money save time and save frustration by helping them choose the right products for their natural hair.

One of the most common questions I'm asked is "How do I choose the right products for my hair?"

This summer, I sent a survey to the natural hair group I founded and asked them to share their top issues related to hair products. The overwhelming response resonated in two areas (1) cost and (2) effectiveness. They told me that they were tired of spending money trying to find the right products. Moreover, they reported, most of the products they bought didn't do what they said they would do or they didn't work because they just didn't know what they needed. I developed a workshop to address their issues and realized there that there was another element to this. Women at the event also wanted to know how to identify their hair type/texture and I was asked to help them understand ingredients.

We spend so much money on products that don't work. Why is this happening? First of all, we have too many choices and it's time to know how to narrow them down. Second, we have the wrong expectations. It's time to reset the way we think about choosing products. Finally, many of us don't know our hair well enough and we don't know what we need. This project is an attempt to help set women with natural hair at ease, to empower them to make better choices that will save them money and hopefully, to get them to the place where they can ROCK their hair however they want.

Chapter One: Time to Reset Expectations

My Hair won't Do That

Do you have the right expectations? What do you actually know about your hair? For many of the women that venture out in the journey of natural hair, hair is a mystery. We certainly know how we want it to look. Oh yeah, we have PhDs in finished hairstyles. We see images every single day; we bump into women on the street and admire their hair. We call girlfriends to discuss so-and-so's hair and Lord knows we get more than enough ideas about how we want our hair to look from TV and magazines. Yes, we are good at that.

And so, we set out on this quest of achieving "her" looks. We want to mimic "her" hair. We admire "her" beauty and then we get motivated to duplicate "her" hairstyle.

In the natural hair community, it happens every day. I believe the epidemic is even worse here because we've jumped out on a limb called "going natural" and we are starting from scratch. We have a clean slate – literally. We have chosen to forego chemicals and now we have all of this...hair. Some of us have the naturally curly locks that bend and move independently. Most of the people who will read this book, however, have been blessed with the course, stiff, kinky texture that just wants to grow and bend. Yes, most of us have a big job on our hands.

This is a colossal problem that has to be addressed if for no other reason than our appearance has a heavy weighting on who we are. African American women disproportionately spend more money on our hair and how we look than any other ethnic group. The Black hair care industry is a $684 million dollar industry with a projection to hit $761 million by 2017. The natural hair community has grown such that sales of chemical relaxers have steadily declined since 2008. Moreover, while we learn to manage our newly natural mane, most will invest in wigs and weaves until we figure out our product regimens and styling routines.

There is Hope

The tipping point for women with natural hair to find happiness and satisfaction with their hair is when they get to know how their hair works. It sounds weird, I know. The truth, for me, is that when I started experimenting, playing with products and working on my styling techniques, I felt a mental release. I finally knew what it felt like to "Rock" my natural hair. I learned how to manipulate it to achieve whatever style I wanted. I figured out what my hair would do and what my hair didn't like. That came after a period of trial, error and documentation. I actually studied my hair.

Knowing my hair allowed me to reset my expectations. I felt more accomplished and surer of myself once I mastered my natural hair. I was at ease with my look, which increased my confidence in many areas of my life. And it helped me settle into a healthy admiration of other women with natural hair. I can look at pictures and images all day and appreciate the beauty of natural hair without the negative jealousy or hair envy. If I see a woman with neat, spiral curls falling down to her shoulders, I'm happy for her. Can I achieve spiral curls on my shoulders, sure, with a weave – and that's okay too. The point is that my mental and emotional health around my hair expectations is set. I'm happy to sport my fro, my chunky twists or whatever other style I choose. I know my hair and I appreciate every kinky, coily strand.

The Work to Achieve Healthy Hair

You have to understand two facts about natural hair. The first thing to know is that length is determined by two things: DNA and maintenance. Your DNA is set when you're born and it is uncontrollable. It is responsible for how fast your hair will grow. That's one aspect. The other aspect is retention – or retaining what you've grown. You can only maintain the hair that you grow by taking care of it which means learning how to maintain (or manage) your hair. You only have control over retention. So you retain the hair you grow by having a routine that includes proper hair care. You can't fix your hair and forget it like you do with relaxed hair.

That means that you have to spend quality time getting to know your hair. With natural hair, you have to learn how it works and learn how to take care of it. And it takes a lot more time than it did with relaxed hair. It is an experience that you should look forward to. Taking the time to understand your hair is a personal endeavor that gives you an opportunity to really love on yourself. I believe it to be intimate and reflective at times. We all know how very important our appearance is to us so taking this opportunity is strengthening in some ways.

The Journey Requires a Process

Have you been documenting your natural hair journey? Are you using a journal? When you spend money on a hair product and it performs well do you record that? Have you found a technique for braiding or twisting that gave you perfect results? On the other hand, are you running through one product and moving onto another never taking time to document that it worked or that it didn't work?

Do you have a hair regimen that may only change based on the time of year or changing climate? That's also important in terms of setting the right expectations. We have to know our hair so well that we know what routines it requires. And we have to know when to change the routine when it's necessary. Are you a hair whisper? You should be.

Who are Your Gurus?

I have long said that YouTube can either set you up to win or set you up to lose based on how you use it. If you are following a hair Guru who doesn't have the same hair texture and hair profile as you do then you are losing. How can you expect your hair to look like someone else's if you have completely different hair? A survey done by Naturallycurly.com reported that the 3C hair type, referring to women with naturally curly hair is the minority. Most of the natural hair community is filled with women with Type 4C hair. In addition, 4C hair types are the kinkiest, most tightly coiled texture. I call it cotton candy hair.

Expectations can also be thrown off by where you get the rest of your information. It has been reported that 81% of online readers trust what bloggers write and 61% will make a purchase based on what they've recommended. Beware of Instagram and Pinterest and Google if you are browsing pictures of women with natural hair that are attractive but don't look like your hair. There is a fine line between being able to appreciate pictures of women with natural hair and admire their hair and being able to achieve their hairstyles. We can't have everything we see.

Find Sources that Make Sense for You

As you are learning your hair and how to appreciate it, learn how to take pride in what you have. Not in trying to have what some other woman has. Embrace your beauty and you are going to be so much more satisfied. We have a habit of wanting to consume what we see and emulate it as opposed to appreciating it like art. That's how I see natural hair. It is an art. It is to be appreciated. However, I cannot expect that I can transform myself into every piece of art. I am my own art. That transformation requires that we do the work mentally, emotionally and literally. This guide will walk you through the fundamentals of this journey. Commit to do the work and you will gain the satisfaction of knowing what your hair wants and needs.

CHAPTER ONE CHECKLIST

- Evaluate your expectations for your natural hair.
- Commit to get to know your hair.
- Choose to follow the appropriate natural hair experts online.

Chapter Two: Getting to Know your Hair

Information Overload

While writing this book, I performed a search on Google for natural hair blogs and it came back with 8.2 million results. We are fortunate and unfortunate to have this growing community. On the positive side, there are many women earning substantial income by sharing their thoughts and documenting their journeys for us online. The marketplace has produced solopreneurs, which means families and communities are thriving and their talent is being recognized. I am happy for this and I feel proud of the women I see making a name for themselves for the cause of natural hair. There is, however, a down side, most of which is information overload. See, there are no barriers to entry in this blogging phenomenon. I can say that with ease. I am a blogger too. My site, www.thewaytonaturalhair.com started as a way to document my journey for the community I created in Indianapolis. So, I won't be a hypocrite here. The truth is that it's so easy to start a blog that they can't all be trusted. You have to beware of conflicting information and just overall bad sources.

Most blog readers are looking for quick, simple answers. To learn natural hair, that's just impossible. There is no "one size fits all" tag here. That is the antithesis of how it works. We may want to speed past the trial and error phase because we have to face the world every day and present ourselves. Most don't have the luxury of hiding away at home to figure out this hair thing.

How Well do you Know Your Hair?

What's your hair type? I propose that there is a lot of information out there about hair typing that separates women into sides. You will find a common theme throughout this book and that is my belief that information has to be validated. A preacher once preached a sermon called "Take the meat and leave the bone." It resonated with me and I applied that philosophy to several areas of my life over the years. To me it says that in terms of hair typing, there may be something valuable that doesn't divide us. Let's find out what's valuable about it and use it. We don't have to agree to the entire philosophy or system.

The most talked about hair typing system in the natural hair community is the Andre Walker system. It covers four main categories plus several subcategories of hair. The system is primarily based on texture. Type one is straight hair. Type two is wavy hair. Type three is curly hair. And type four is coily or zigzag hair. In most cases in our community, we work with either Type 3 or type 4 hair. I believe that it's okay to use the Andre Walker system as a basis for understanding. There's nothing wrong with having a reference point. If I know that my hair is tightly coiled with a zigzag pattern then I also know that it might be safe to listen to advice from other women with tight coils and zigzag patterns concerning styling techniques and sometimes products. That's fine. I know I cannot take advice from women with naturally curly hair because I simply don't have that type of hair. And that's all I really need to get from the Andre Walker system.

Realize this. When you try to style your hair against what it naturally wants to do you must be ready to put in extra work. That should emphasize why it is so important to get to know your own hair. Learning what your hair actually wants to do means you're going to have a lot less work and you'll be much happier.

What is it you actually need to know about your hair to make the best product choices?

In order to be a smarter consumer I believe you need to know your Natural Hair Profile™. The

NHP is a summary of natural hair data and or characteristics that are critical to making decisions about which products to buy. I believe you need to know texture not necessarily type. I believe you need to understand porosity. And I believe that you need to know your elasticity. There are other attributes that will come into play but they don't make as much of an impact as your texture, your porosity, and your elasticity.

What is the Natural Hair Profile™

The NHP is simply a set of facts about your hair. The determination was created after years of study and researching the things I needed to know about my hair above everything else. When I have taught workshops all over my state and spoken to hundreds of women, I have helped them problem solve by asking questions about these particular features. I found that knowing these characteristics were 90% of the reason I was making good choices for my hair. By

24

understanding the texture, porosity and elasticity of your natural hair I believe you save time and money when choosing products and I think it relieves you of a great deal of frustration when you don't get the results you want.

The texture of your hair is defined by whether your hair is loose or tight on a scale. Loose hair is straight and silky. Tight hair is usually course and has extreme shrinkage. You can determine this by the feel of your hair and by the look of your hair. If you have several different textures on your hair that's fine. That's actually normal. You will want to pay attention to the majority texture on your head if you have more than one.

Porosity is the ability for your hair strands to hold moisture. Your porosity is either low to high on the scale. You can determine your level of porosity by doing a porosity test. That's where you take a strand of clean dry hair and place it in a glass of water that is luke warm. If your hair strand dives to the bottom of the glass then your hair is highly porous. If they hair strand seems to float at the top of the water then you have low elasticity. Porosity really sets the tone for what products to choose for your natural hair.

Elasticity is the primary indicator of the strength of your natural hair strands. It is important to determine elasticity because you may need more reconstructors and protein-based products to add strength to your hair as opposed to moisturizing products.

In summary, your Natural Hair Profile™ is going to be extremely important to understand about your hair, far more than hair type. Your Natural Hair Profile™ is going to save you money and time in getting the results you want. You'll get the hairstyles you like once you understand your Natural Hair Profile™ and make product buying decisions based on it. We will discuss the NHP throughout the book in greater detail.

CHAPTER TWO CHECKLIST

- Be willing to look for appropriate sources of information.
- Understand your Natural Hair Profile™.

Chapter Three: Getting to Know Hair Products

Do You Know How Products Work?

When we had relaxed hair and we would go see our stylists, there are many of us who sat in the chair and literally 'relaxed'. We let our hairdresser do whatever he/she wanted and we really didn't question them. We had a 'fix it and forget it' mindset. Half the time we didn't even know what products they were using in our hair. We just trusted them.

Natural hair requires more work on the front end to save us time and money on the back end. We can't take things for granted like we did with relaxed hair because we're working with raw clay so to speak. Part of that learning process is figuring out how products work. In this section, we'll discuss the three main categories of products we use for our natural hair namely;

cleansers, conditioners and styling products. We'll identify the most common characteristics and then we'll dive into ingredients that make up these products. Understand that this is not an exhaustive review. People earn cosmetology licenses and chemical degrees to cover this topic. Major brands pay a great deal of money to scientists and marketing departments to create and sell hair products. We are a part of a potentially trillion-dollar industry. What you'll learn here is what you need to know to make the best buying decisions for your natural hair.

What do they do?

SHAMPOO BASICS

- A good shampoo should cleanse your scalp to make it healthy and make your hair easier to comb through thereby conditioning it. A healthy scalp isn't one where you've stripped away all of your natural oils. That is a big misnomer.

- Shampoo has three main ingredients (1) a surfactant to dissolve oils and dirt (2) a cationic conditioner to offset frizz and (3) a pH balancer to keep the cuticle intact.

CONDITIONING BASICS

- The main job of a conditioner is to detangle the hair strands. It softens each individual strand so that it moves freely from the others.
- The main ingredients in conditioners are (1) emollients and (2) cationics.
- Emollients form film on hair and acts like a lubricant that provides slip. They will flatten the cuticle (the outer layer) of the strand to make it look shiny and some will even penetrate the hair to improve its elasticity. And they seal in moisture.
- Cationics condition the hair and offset frizz as mentioned earlier.

- Deep conditioners may house a third ingredient like hydrolyzed proteins, which work to strengthen hair.

Why are Emollients so Important?

Emollients have a huge role to play in the life of a Naturalista. Because our hair has a predisposition to be dry just based on how it grows out of our heads, we work around the clock to redeposit moisture. If you're like me then you know that we go to great lengths to make sure that nothing that comes into contact with our hair will dry it out and we work to keep our moisture intact. A few years ago, I went online researching small businesses on Etsy looking to find all of these great, silk lined hats only to find out later that the local department store had plenty. That's how worried I was about drying out my hair. Choosing the right emollients can mean the difference in healthy hair vs. dry brittle hair that breaks easily. If you choose an emollient that is too heavy then it will weigh your hair down. Too light? That might give you frizzy hair. Common emollients are natural butters, oils and silicones.

How many Stylers have you tried?

Curl booster, curly enhancer, curl quenchers, curly definers, curl keepers? The number of styling products is almost obnoxious. Literally every day I'm alerted to a new company selling products to the natural hair community. I make it my business to know, so I know. What's encouraging is the amount of attention we receive. At the rate of money we spend companies who want our business certainly should court us. The problem is that there is no real qualifier when a product hits a shelf. Anybody can make natural hair products and it seems at times that everybody does.

That said, it is imperative that you understand what's being sold.

Styling products are important to our regimen. They determine how we present our hair to the world. They are the basis of our hairstyles. We want either tiny curls or big waves. We like smooth straight natural hair or we want sculpted updos. And some of us even want the flexibility to go back and forth. I personally have paid the equivalent of a year's salary trying to master a Wash and Go Style. Whatever it is we desire, we've learned that our styling products are the vehicles to get us there. And product manufacturers and their marketing departments have ensured we have plenty of choices. At last count, African American women were spending millions of dollars on hair care and the number is steadily increasing.

How do they work?

STYLING BASICS

- Styling products produce film on the hair to shape it

- They create bonds amongst the strands to curl them, bend them, lay them down or define them
- Gels distribute ingredients known as polymers, a plastic (PVP) to attract to itself and hold hair in a fixed shape. The second critical ingredient is a carbomer, a synthetic that thickens the product. The effectiveness of the gel is based on its formula and the climate.
- Custards, Puddings and Jellies usually moisturize and often times they define. If you want hold, look for carbomers and polymers in the ingredient list.
- Hair butters are usually plant-based emollients that rinse out easily with water.
- Hair milks/lotions add moisture to hair primarily with the use of water as the main ingredient.

Ingredients in Hair Products are either Natural or Synthetic

It's important to understand that products that say they're natural aren't necessarily so. Only a USDA label ensures it's organic. Due to the amount of large and small companies making hair products these days it makes sense to be aware of the types of ingredients going into your hair. In the case of larger companies, cosmetic scientists or cosmetic chemists usually make the decisions about formulas. These individuals are educated in the field of chemistry and have a great deal of expertise in terms of testing and engineering the right formula to produce a product claim. They do this by using natural ingredients in some cases. For the most part, however, they achieve their goals by creating synthetic ingredients.

When you're looking at labels in most cases you'll find ingredients that you can't pronounce. That is actually true with many of the hair and skin care products you'll pick up on the shelves. I want to caution you right now that you shouldn't run from a product just because there are big words on the labels. Each of the ingredients has a job to do. Until you know what role the ingredients play, don't be afraid of them. We've gotten so caught up in the list of "No" ingredients that we haven't even figured out how our hair will respond to something. Take a step back and think about that. My husband reacts badly to milk. It sours his stomach. Does that mean I should avoid it too? Not to mention the fact that the very ingredients we run from in hair products are being used in our skincare. The point is that until you know for yourself that something is ineffective for your hair strands, why are you letting the marketplace limit your choices? According to researchers, the hair care space has become such big business that manufacturers are working diligently to influence our buying decisions.

The point here is that we already trust cosmetic scientists with the products we use on our faces, our bodies and in the case of food, we lean on scientists as well. I don't believe in shying away from a hair product because it uses ingredients with a "bad reputation". Everything mixed is meant to do a specific job based on that company's claim.

Should You Really Stay Away from Silicones?

- Silicones are lightweight emollients.
- They coat the hair to be slicker and smoother.
- They add shine.
- They prevent proteins and moisturizes from penetrating
- Cosmetic scientists produce them.

Examples of ingredients with scary names that just might work for you:

- Dimethicone – an emollient
- Citric acid – a pH balancer
- Stearyl alcohol – emollient
- Cetrimonium Bromide – a cationic conditioner

Major Ingredient Categories that Matter (In no particular order)

Surfactants – cleansing agents/detergents. Examples: sodium lauryl sulphate.

Foam Boosters – produce foam. Example: DEA.

Conditioning agents – soften and reduce static charge. Examples: silicones, polymers, quatimium 80.

pH Balancers – balance the pH in water based products. Example: citric acid.

Humectants – attract moisture into hair strands. Examples: propylene glycol, PEG-, sodium PCA.

Thickeners – thicken the product. Examples: guar gum, glycol distearate.

Fatty Alcohols – emulsifiers usually derived from oils like coconut oil. Example: cetyl alcohol.

Preservatives- give product a shelf life. Examples: parabens, benzyl alcohol.

Additives (natural and synthetic) - enhance the product. Examples: vitamins, proteins, botanical extracts.

Emollients – lubricate strands and detangle. Examples: silicones, oils, butters, hydrolyzed proteins.

Moisturizers – add moisture. Example: glycerin.

This list of ingredients and their roles is meant to put you at ease for picking products. As I stated before, there are hundreds and hundreds of product ingredients, far too many to cover here. My hope is that you'd have a firm understanding of what these ingredients are meant to do for your natural hair. The roles that they play help ensure you get a product that is not only effective but easy to use and pleasant to work with. Take control of your product experience.

CHAPTER THREE CHECKLIST

- Spend time learning about the different product types and their roles.
- Recognize natural vs. synthetic ingredients.
- Seek out the major ingredient categories on product labels.

Chapter Four: Finding out What you Need

Do you Know what you Need for your Hair?

Finding the best ingredients for your natural hair will depend on you knowing what your hair needs. It's going to depend on your texture your porosity and your elasticity above all else. These make up what I call the Natural Hair Profile™. I think curl pattern and density and the thickness of your hair will play a part but you have to know the basics first. Understanding the pH of products is worth understanding too but in most cases the manufacturers have already sorted that out for you. Find the time to learn how your hair works in order to be satisfied with the results from the hairstyling you desire.

What the NHP Tells you about Buying Products

In general, there are some rules that you should follow in terms of buying products based on your Natural Hair Profile™.

Is your hair texture curly or is it coily? Is your porosity high or is it low? Do you have high elasticity or is your hair's elasticity low?

Hair Texture

I believe that texture will determine the amount of products you need to use. If you have curly hair then you're generally going to need fewer products. That's because your hair naturally wants to generate individual curls. That is not the case with coily or zigzag textures. If your hair is more coily then you're going to need more products to get it to stay in the desired mode and to define the curl. Most of us want our hair to be curly and we want to show curl patterns so that it is defined. For someone with a zigzag texture that will involve using more products.

Hair Porosity

The porosity of your hair will determine the protein/moisture balance in the products you buy. In other words your hair's porosity will tell you if you need to buy products with more moisture or more protein until you can get it balanced. Having high porosity is like having shingles missing from your roof and a leaking basement. Moisture can move very easily in and out of the hair strands. Sealing in moisture with the right products is critical. This attribute also requires regular protein to rebuild the hair's structure. With low porosity, it is also hard to moisturize hair but for a different reason. If you have low porosity that means that your hair is like Fort Knox. It takes a great deal of work to break through the walls of your hair strand to get to the cortex and give it proper hydration. You will need a high degree of moisturizing products in your regimen. You will have to have moisture from the shampoo stage all the way through to the conditioning and styling phases. In addition, even your daily regimen has to involve moisture. You possibly have the driest hair along the spectrum.

A product with a moisture/protein balance is critical depending on your porosity. Protein will help you rebuild your hair strand adding some strength and moisturizing products will obviously help you to combat the dryness. The best care for hair on either end of the spectrum is to treat it extremely well. You will want more deep conditioning treatments. You may want more trips to the salon. However, you have to care for your hair using both proteins and moisture.

Hair Elasticity

Knowing the elasticity of your hair will alert you to whether you buy products that are more complicated. Therefore, if your hair has high elasticity that means that it will really want to bounce back. In that case products with simple curl activators will accommodate your needs. You're not going to have to do very much work because your hair wants to curl. With low elasticity, your hair has no snapback. That means that you're going to have to do two things. You're going to have to add protein treatments to resolve the elasticity issue and you're going to want to use curl defining jellies or curly puddings with polymers to show off the definition. I caution you not to get overly complex with your Natural Hair Profile™. Accept where you are, evaluate where you are and then go about the work. Your ultimate desire is to have healthy natural hair, right? That means that you're going to have to do a little work to get it into a healthy state. It is possible to have a balanced Natural Hair Profile™. It simply requires your attention. You don't have to start over again.

If you aren't sure where you stand with your hair at all, **download my FREE Healthy Hair Checklist at www.naturalhairindy.com**. It's a simple and easy way to find out if you're making the right choices with your natural hair.

CHAPTER FOUR CHECKLIST

- Know your hair texture.
- Test your hair's porosity and elasticity.
- Have a plan to improve moisture and protein levels.

Chapter Five: Picking Products

How do you Narrow Down the Choices?

Are there too many products in this space? Yes, the truth is that there are too many product choices in the natural hair community. It's getting worse every day. Although it sounds like a good thing that we have so much attention from product manufacturers within the industry the truth is that it just makes it more difficult to make smart choices. I watched a Ted talk recently where a psychologist talked about the fact that once someone has too many choices they can sometime shut down. In our case we don't shut down, we simply buy more. The term is product junkie, right? I think that can be a problem and I think that it gets expensive overtime. Who has money to buy products that will just sit on your shelf until the next product swap?

And there are women mixing up products in their kitchens every single day and selling them in the marketplace. There's nothing wrong with that. Look at Lisa Price with Carol's Daughter. I love the fact that women entrepreneurs are being birthed out of this need to learn our hair and to find products that work. I'm proud of that. The problem is that we have to know how to discern all of these choices. We have to know how to shop. When you walk into a department store in the shoe section, you typically have an idea in mind of what works for you. You know the colors that you typically like to buy you know the heel sizes that you like, you already have shoes at home, and you consider them when you buy new shoes. For some reason when it comes to buying hair products none of the same logic applies. We just go hog wild.

So how do you pick?

Start with a Formula

I suggest you start with a formula. Look at the brands, first; the product lines within the brands next and then study the labels. When you study the labels look at the claims.

Brands ➔ Product Lines ➔ Labels ➔ Claims

 In looking at the brands, I'd suggest you chose those that are familiar and that you've heard about the most first. No disrespect to the brand-new products that are hitting the market every day. There's nothing wrong with supporting those companies. I certainly do but I also know my hair extremely well.   I just believe that you'll want to start building a regimen around brands that are easy to find due to the fact that you're going to test things out many times before you determine your hair's favorites.   Secondly, look at the products within their product line. Typically, everybody has a shampoo, a conditioner or maybe several plus they'll have styling products. Usually there's oil and there's some kind of spray. Start with that. Try your product line and see if they can satisfy your needs. Do they have one thing that works and one thing that doesn't? That's okay. Document your findings in a journal.

How do you Evaluate the Claims?

Evaluation takes place based on knowledge of your hair first and of ingredients second. Luckily, from reading this book so far, you know more about your Natural Hair Profile™ plus you know how to identify ingredients that work and you know why they work because you know what they do. From there, you want to line things up.

1. What does the product claim it will do? Does it help to curl your hair? Does it help to moisturize your hair? Start with that.
2.   The next thing you want to do is to look at the ingredients and find out if those ingredients support the claim. You know

what makes a product define, you know what makes a product soften and you know what makes a product moisturize.

3. Read the directions next. Do the directions lineup with what you know about your hair and about the products. Do the directions tell you to apply on dry hair or wet hair? That tells you something about whether or not it's going to be able to do what it promises.

4. The last thing you are going to want to do is to document. This is where you are going to get your journal out and you're going to make note of the day, the weather, your steps and you are going to make note of the amounts of the product that you use. I'm a strong believer that you cannot make a decision about whether or not a product works only by using it one time. Test the products two to three times. Document the conditions and document the outcomes.

Do you like it? Great, now you need to know the common denominators. At the end of the day, you need to be able to have a Gold Star ingredients list. This list will tell you exactly what your hair loves and picking products with your Gold Stars will make your life so much easier.

This process is easy and it becomes routine once you've done it a few times.

 Just think like a scientist. You'll want to isolate the variables meaning you can't test everything at one time. Find your ideal shampoo and conditioner combo and then begin to work on the stylers. Know your ideal outcome for every product you evaluate. Are you looking to reduce frizz, hold curls or help with manageability? Identify your need before you begin. And keep a set of rules to be fair to the competing products. If you keep a deep conditioner in your hair for 30 minutes for product A then do the same for product B.

Lastly, make a decision. You love the product because it did what you wanted or you hate it and it needs to be given away to somebody else. Be clear. Even commercially made products shouldn't sit on the shelf for years and years. Was it so-so? Move on until you find something your hair loves.

The Big Four Ingredient Types

Remember the big four ingredient types. Think about ingredients and group them to make them easy to evaluate. Determine which are moisturizers, humectants, emollients and reconstructors. Moisturizers are there to improve elasticity. The more elastic your hair is the less breakage you're going to experience. Moisturizers should typically be added daily depending on your Natural Hair Profile™ and the environment you live in. The next thing you want to think about is humectants. Humectants are going to pull moisture in from one area to another

53

area. They are great for humid and moist conditions. In dry air, humectants are going to pull moisture out of your hair so keep that in mind when you're reading the labels. Emollients are not moisturizers but they work closely with moisturizers. They're going to seal moisture that's already there. You'll see plenty of emollients on your product labels. They will be things like Shea butter, olive oil and jojoba oil as well as silicones. Lastly, look for reconstructors. These are products that contain protein. A very common reconstructor is hydrolyzed protein. They will build the hair and may harden it too so be careful here.

Reading Product Labels

Evaluating claims also requires that you know how to read labels beyond the basics. Most of us already know that we should look at the top five ingredients on a product label. That's common knowledge. What I suggest though is that you go beyond just the top five. Did you know that the top one third of the product ingredients represents 90 to 95% of the product itself? You know more now about identifying ingredients so you don't have to be scared of those ingredients with the difficult names. You're going to know what works for your hair whether the ingredient was created by a cosmetic scientist or by nature. The bottom one third of the product ingredient list represents only 3% of the product. That means you don't have to freak out if you see fragrances or perfume at the end of the list. They are not making or breaking the product. They have very little effect.

I've said it once but I will say it again here; you have to know your Natural Hair Profile™ before you can get to this point. You will not make a good decision about buying products and evaluating products unless you know your hair. The texture of your hair will tell you the amount of products you need; the porosity will the protein/moisture balance you need and your elasticity will give you details for adding reconstructors or products that are more specialized.

So, what do you do when you get home with your products? There are three steps you want to make. Read the claims, evaluate the claims and document the outcomes. That is how you test products and that is how you build a regimen for your hair.

CHAPTER 5 CHECKLIST

- Think about how you shop for products.
- Start to build a regimen that includes the products that work well for your hair.
- Read a product's claim and know how to ˈ test it.

Chapter Six: Additional Resources

Are there Tools to Help?

It is well known that the amount of information floating out in cyberspace about natural hair is more than enough. It can be downright ridiculous. For about the last 7 or 8 years Naturalistas have dominated the web sharing pictures and telling their journeys. There is a certain amount of pride when one demystifies their natural hair and most feel compelled to teach what they know. I know this firsthand. You're reading my eBook (smile). Although it is encouraging to see women master their manes, it also causes a pool of experts that we have to swim through to find out what applies to us.

I've long said to my group of Naturalistas that they should beware the amount of information online. There are far too many experts with glitzy blogs and fancy YouTube channels to be caught up in. I believe that if you want to follow the advice of vloggers and bloggers then at least find ones who have hair similar to yours. For example, I have kinky, tightly coiled hair. It is not naturally defined. I call it cotton candy hair. So if I want to find a guru online for advice, there is no reason I should follow a Naturalista with loose curls. She is going to get different results with a hair product every time. Her application of the product will be different and the amount of products that she uses will be different. No, I need to find a subject matter expert with kinky, tightly coiled hair to follow. Make sense?

Uncovering tools to help is critical to making good decisions about products. I believe there are some awesome resources to tap into that cost little to no money at all.

Seek Professionals

Stylists are a mixed bag when it comes to being able to make product decisions with you. These people are professional licensed cosmetologists who have invested in their education to be able to manage and style your hair. In some cases, they gain knowledge about products based on the salon they choose to work in. You'll find them loyal to certain brands and in some cases they are bound to suggest only certain brands based on the agreements they've made in their salons. It is rare that you'll find a stylist who knows a great deal about a plethora of products. Of course, if you do find her, hold onto her. She is valuable. Unfortunately, this is not normally the case.

Groups in Your Community

Meetups provide another path to finding out good information. Natural hair events are occurring all over the world and they are usually organized by caring women who want to get you to the information you need to make smart decisions about your hair. In some cases, they'll even offer product swaps. These are activities where attendees bring in gently used products that may not have worked for their hair to exchange with another woman in the same predicament. Both parties walk away with a new (to them) product to try at home.

Apps for Natural Hair

A newer, lesser-known option to take the guesswork out of picking products is your smartphone. I've long been a fan of using Apps to save time and money in my personal life. Everywhere you turn, there's a new App promising to make our lives easier. The first natural hair App I ever downloaded was one developed by Naturallycurly.com called Curls on the Go. It was useful then and it's still useful today. Since then, I've made it my business to scan the iTunes store every few weeks to find new tools for natural hair. Today, I have about 18 although not all of them help with products. The Apps I believe you'll find useful for choosing the right products for your hair list these features:

- Active forums that offer product reviews (Curls on the Go)
- Videos with product reviews and ingredient lists (The Natural Community)
- Glossary and regimen calendar to track results (Know Your Hair)
- Product Brands with links to their sites (Naturally Me)

Understand that Apps can come and go quickly. There were a few more I wanted to list at the beginning of this project and they are no longer around. Lean on them while you can especially while you're in this learning mode. Once you discover how to pick the right products and how they'll work in your natural hair then you won't need as many tools.

CHAPTER SIX CHECKLIST

- Consult professionals in your area for help with your hair.

- Leverage natural hair groups to share information.
- Check out the various smart phone apps dedicated to natural hair.

Tales of a Former Product Junkie (And How I Got Set Free)

It is part of the human condition to be drawn to things. We are wired that way. Everybody in your life probably has a habit or an obsession with something. Think about it. We live in a world where it is absolutely normal to be a crazed fanatic. There are sports fanatics, shoe fanatics, music lovers, foodies, Gamers, Gamblers and Product Junkies. Yes, Product Junkies.

Hello. My name is Darice and I am a Product Junkie.

It's comforting to know that part of solving a problem is admitting that you have one. I'm on my way to healing and restoration. For real.

In the Beginning

Initially, I started my love affair with hair products purely from a healthy place. It was my second

Big Chop and I was determined to learn my hair. Blame it on my controlling personality but I refused to look crazy and I felt like if I just invested some time into getting to know my natural hair then I could achieve the looks I wanted. A major part of that process was sorting through hair products.

I set about going from one product line to the next documenting what worked. I paid attention to how the product looked, smelled, the consistency, the claim and whether it did what it was supposed to do. When something worked, I noted the ingredients. When a product failed, I noted the ingredients. I kept a master list.

And once I "mastered" my natural hair and discovered which products worked I kept buying new products.

This time, I was buying products for the good of the team. Or at least, that's what I told myself. I was just starting to connect with other women with natural hair, women I called Naturalistas. And so as we swapped stories, and hair woes, we'd naturally discuss hair products. Never wanting to be left out of the conversation, when someone mentioned a product I hadn't used, I went to buy it. The slight obsession began.

As my natural hair journey progressed, I became more product-obsessed. Subscription boxes not only fueled my desires, they poured gasoline on the problem. I could sample new products every month at a reasonable cost AND they were delivered right to my door! Oh my Goodness, was I happy. The Curlboxes and Curlkits of the world led me to discover brands as they hit the market and if I received a sample size that I really liked, I'd go searching for the full size.

The slight obsession became a Full Blown Crazy Lady Fest!

Enter my Tribe

At this point, the Product Junkie Queen (me) had convinced herself that the knowledge of products was a strength and not a weakness. I had founded a group called the Naturalistas in Nap in my city of Indianapolis and we'd grown quickly. Hundreds of women were attending my workshops and events and learning more about their hair. I could literally prescribe a product if someone told me that they were having an issue. Like, seriously, I knew that much about what was on the market and natural hair that I could call off a product by name and brand if I was asked for a recommendation. I was a circus act. Step right up and meet the Incredible Crazy Product Junkie Lady!

Seriously.

I had gone off a cliff into Crazy-Ville over natural hair products and I learned how far I had gone by watching my group, the Naturalistas.

After about a year of events I started to send out group surveys to get feedback and to solicit ideas for planning purposes. Two things struck me into realizing that being a Product Junkie was not okay.

1. My group kept requesting that we hold product swaps at our events. Now for those of you reading this who are unfamiliar, I'll explain. A product swap is an activity where people bring in hair products that are gently used to exchange with others. The idea is that you get rid of products that didn't work for you and try something new. Some women will look for a product that they already know will work for them at product swaps. At first, it just seemed like a really smart thing to do. Efficient. However, as an event host, you are able to see things that others don't see. And what I saw was a lot of women investing a great deal of money in products

67

that didn't work and continuing to do so. It was pretty sobering.

2. The second phenomena I realized from surveying was how many women were searching year after year for the right products. It was year 3 of our group's existence when it all came about and I decided that in order to lead Naturalistas to a better place in their hair journey and give them some financial relief and stress relief, we all had to get better with products. And so, I gave up my gluttonous hair product ways.

Lead by Example

There are so many problems with being a Product Junkie.

- The expense. When I was buying all of those hair products and subscribing to companies to send me products I did so telling myself that it was okay because I was no longer going to regular hair appointments. See, many Naturalistas choose the path of natural hair and are left to fend for themselves. There is a great lack of trained professionals ready to take care of our hair so we become DIY stylists. And yes, most of us master saving that money and applying it to good. I, however, applied it to the obsession of hair products. And hair products outweighed what I would have spent otherwise. I wonder, now, what I could have invested in and how much it would have grown to.

- Hair suffers. Another observation I made from hosting events month after month is the number of women whose hair was not growing and who were not maintaining their hair well. They simply weren't making any progress with their natural hair. And how could they? They were hopping from product to product trying to fix issues with their hair, so how could it grow or get better? If you had a medical ailment you wouldn't go see a different doctor every week you'd stick with one diagnosis and see it through before you jumped ship for poor results. But I was watching women trek all of these products to events to swap and asking the same questions during Q&A about their hair. I know that there are those who can try new products without long term damage. I am one of those women but I've also done a crazy amount of work on my own natural hair so I'm comfortable. I know how to rebound when a product goes wrong and add extra care to my hair regimen. So if you can get to know your hair and understand how it works then you can feel free to try new products from time to time because you know how to evaluate and still grow healthy hair. Unfortunately, this is not the norm.

- Wasted time and money. If you have played the Product Junkie Game then I'm willing to bet you've also invested a small fortune on your hair. Products range in price from low to high like everything else but Product Junkies rarely set a standard for how much money they'll spend to try something new. As a matter of fact, price is no object to most if the promise is attractive enough. Oh, that conditioner fights frizz? Well I need to try that! The only objection you hear from a Product Junkie is over how long it will take for the product to be delivered…and the cost of shipping, maybe. And for those investing the money, they're also investing time. You know how it is. You put something in your hair, it fails, and you have to start the wash routine all over again. It ain't pretty. Not at all.

Breaking the Spell

Being a Product Junkie is like being put under a magical spell. We are lulled into thinking that buying and trying a new hair product makes us feel good somehow. There is a mystery behind that pretty label and that shiny bottle that we want to get to know. We want to test it, smell it, spray it and pour it. The products are alluring and we get some sense of achievement or satisfy a sense of curiosity.

The reality is that our attention has been misplaced. We have gotten used to trying to achieve hair nirvana only through the use of products when products are only part of the solution. We also need to consider hair care and hair knowledge. Hair care is important because nothing matters if you can't keep your hair from shedding, splitting and falling out. Hair knowledge sets the stage for what to buy, how much to buy and how products work. And so products are only the third most important part of the equation. Hair care and knowledge of hair come first.

Test, Record, Keep it or Give it Away

Breaking the Product Junkie trance requires that you turn your attention back to the basics. Mastering the basics allows you the opportunity to love your natural hair from a healthy place of experimentation. And the basics involve finding your perfect set of Holy Grail products and Gold Star ingredients.

Holy Grail products are your "ride or die" products. They are the ones that you KNOW will never fail your hair. You can use them and get the perfect balance of moisture and protein. Your hair is strong and pliable. You have no scalp condition or irritations. You don't suffer from shedding or breakage and you see regular growth. These are the products you want to buy in bulk and keep on your shelves. You trust them.

Within those Holy Grail products are your Gold Star ingredients. The ingredients in hair products that your hair loves and agrees with. When you see these in other products, you know how they're going to react in your hair because you've learned what they are. You also trust them and they give you a basis for shopping for new products for your natural hair.

You master your hair products and they don't master you.

And with that comes the freedom to shop from a healthy place. Once you've mastered the basics, you can feel free to try new products from time to time understanding what is going to work because you've created a baseline to compare to. I love Product X so if I try Brand Y, I can compare it to X to make an educated decision for my hair. I'm not playing the Product Junkie Game at this point. I am the Product Master! How cool is that?

Find a product that doesn't work for you, fine. There is no stress, no frustration and no leaving nasty comments on the Brands Facebook page. You simply give it away and go back to your Holy Grail products. Everything is alright and you simply move on.

The hypnotic effects of being a Product Junkie are replaced by the soothing effect of mastering your products. It feels good to walk down the product aisle in a store, pick up a bottle, glance at the claim and the ingredients and either shake my head "no" or put it in my shopping cart. I've got this. No more 'Crazy Product Lady' for me. No Sir. Now when I speak or hold a workshop I give less advice about products (although I can still go there) and focus more on hair care and hair knowledge. Products are definitely fun to play with as long as you know the rules of the game.

Are you a Product Junkie?

How many of these Brands do you have in your Cabinet? (Sorted by Price)

Low Cost < $10

Cantu	Beautiful Texture	Nothing But
Eden Bodyworks	Au Natural	Elasta QP
Crème of Nature	Aunt Jackie's	Curls Unleashed

Mid-Range $11-19

Alikay Naturals	As I Am	Curls
Design Essentials	Hydratherma Naturals	Miss Jessie
My Honey	Obia	Soultanicals

Child		
Wondercurl	Komaza Care	

Luxury Brands >$20

Entwine Couture	TreLuxe	Karen's Body Beautiful	Koils by Nature

Wondering how I generated this list? At one point I had every one of these brands in my cabinets.

Getting Started with DIY Products (For those times when you need to fill a Gap in the Market)

Choosing to wear natural hair after relying on chemical relaxers is like going on an adventure. You have to pick a destination which, for most of us, is healthy natural hair. Next you plan a route. I've said many times in this book that the route is your hair care routine, your regimen. In any adventure, you should expect the unexpected. This truth comes to light when the product or technique doesn't work so you regroup, maybe even wash your hair again and start over. We ask for directions on most trips, right? We follow YouTube tutorials, read blogs and head to natural hair events on the natural hair adventure. And sometimes the highlight of an adventure is when you learn how to just wander.

Making your own natural hair products is like wandering around lost (in a good way).

It is an opportunity to play, to experiment and to be pleasantly surprised. It's also very fulfilling when you get it right.

There are several great reasons to get started with Do-it-Yourself hair products

- With more companies and smaller brands offering products, it has become tough to find what works for our hair. Overchoice is a term used to explain when the advantages of having so many choices is overshadowed by the complexity of the decision making process. And it's a real problem in the natural hair product marketplace. Making your own products could eliminate the need to be frustrated and confused.
- The other factor with having so many products on the market is that the offerings

are becoming more alike. There are fewer differentiators between the brands. The same staple products are being sold with similar formulas consisting of the same ingredients. That is normal for mass marketing and that is where the natural hair community is going – toward mass marketing. So by jumping into DIY, you're able to customize something just for you.

- Products being sold online and locally by bigger companies rarely offer natural ingredients. It is not cost effective and less attractive to them. It makes perfect sense, however for you. You are able to make products in smaller batches and use the very best that nature has to offer which is better for your hair.

- You'll have more control over what's being applied to your hair. You can forget about learning product ingredients with names that you can't pronounce, reading labels and testing claims. Making your own products means that you can keep products as simple or as complex as you desire and you determine the final outcome from start to finish.

To be fair, I also have to mention the cons.

Making your own natural hair products is a great deal of work, especially in the beginning. It takes time to figure out what to mix, how much, storage and to test outcomes. When I started many years ago, I spent most nights reading and learning about ingredients. On the weekends, I tested formulas on myself and my very patient family. I made notes of all of the outcomes and would usually have to tweak – a lot.

It can also be expensive to become a Mixtress. There are simple ingredients that you can find in the aisle of your local grocery store and there are the more exotic offerings that have to be ordered online. I am happy that I didn't keep track of how much I spent on product formulas that didn't work. I'd probably be sick right now. Not only did I buy ingredients, I invested a small fortune in tools, containers and books.

And I mentioned time but let me mention it again. There is so much to learn. When I found the right ingredients, I had to play with the ratios. That alone, took hours and days. And it was also important to learn about storage and how long a product could last before it got rancid and had to be thrown away. So I'd make a batch of something and test that aspect as well as the effectiveness. And I also wanted to be able to duplicate formulas that I liked so I'd make the same product over and over again.

Despite the time, money and expense of making your own natural hair products, I will always be a proponent of that practice. The benefits to my hair easily outweigh the costs even today with all of the choices in the marketplace. At any given time that you visit my home, you will always find a moisturizing spray that I've made and use daily.

You'll see oils that I've mixed together to add to store bought products and for oil treatments. And at the very least, you'll find a butter or cream type of twisting agent that I usually double as a skin care treatment. I just believe in DIY products.

So how do you get started?

At a minimum, you can start making your own natural hair products as long as you have some tools, formulas, ingredients and time to test. It also helps if you've surveyed your hair enough to know your Natural Hair Profile™ and you've gathered your Gold Star Ingredient List. If you haven't gotten that far then go back to those chapters, read and do the work. Otherwise, you're going to have a pretty frustrating experience making products.

Tools you'll want to order or find locally include bottles, caps, pumps, sprayers, jars and tins. I ordered many online because the prices were competitive. I used SunburstBottle.com, Medina

Online and FreundContainer.com. These companies don't require a huge volume either so you can order as few as you like.

Formulas to mix hair products are all over the web. I'd beware, however, because not all of the sources offering help understand the science of mixing. I like Pinterest but only after you've thoroughly invested the ingredients. To start, I used online sources like From Nature with Love and Lotioncrafter because they also sold the ingredients and offered sales. There are many books available on Amazon as well.

Ingredients are where you'll spend the most time hunting within this process. In addition to the sites listed above, you can also check for ingredients online at Amazon, Brambleberry and your local organic grocers. You're going to be amazed at the number of choices and prices for shea butter alone. Get ready.

When you're ready to assemble the tools and ingredients, you'll have to test your formulas. There is nothing better than having a journal next to you at all times to document reactions and outcomes. You'll also want to invest in pH strips to ensure you aren't freaking your hair out too much.

The benefits of making your own hair products are rich. There is something amazing and empowering about taking control of your hair care. You'll find it to be easy once you discover ingredients you like and it can also be cheaper because of your batches as long as your storage is good.

Take the time to learn to make products and gain a skill that will provide value for you and your natural hair for years to come.

Quick Tips + Product Recommendations for Natural Hair

In this section I want to address some common issues that Naturalistas deal with on a regular basis. These problems can be resolved from several angles. There is usually a way to solve them using techniques but most times, they can be solved with products. So I want to help by giving you some ingredients to hunt for and products to try. The recommendations are based on my personal experience and research from other Curly Girls plus online reviews. Need more help? Be sure to register to hear about online courses, new books, live events and coaching at www.naturalhairindy.com.

Dry Hair

When it comes to dry hair the key is to use water based products that moisturize. You'll want to refrain from mineral oils or petroleum unless they're being used to seal in moisture. Signs that you're using the wrong product are continuous shedding, breakage and brittle hair. Look for glycol and panthenol on the ingredients list. They bind moisture inside the hair shaft with a protective film. Be prepared to use daily moisturizers in addition to using moisturizing products on wash day (from the shampoo all the way to the deep conditioner).

Ingredients that Matter for Dry Hair

- Water, aloe vera juice
- Humectants
- Penetrating oils and butters to seal after water based products

Recommendations

- My Honey Child O'Honey Curl Mist

- Obia Natural Hair Care Curl Hydration Spray
- Jessicurl Too Shea! Extra Moisturizing Conditioner
- Ouidad Curl Recovery Melt Down Extreme Repair Mask
- Camille Rose Naturals Coconut Water Penetrating Hair Treatment

Frizzy Hair

Several things contribute to frizzy natural hair including product build up and the condition of your cuticle layer. The key is to get your moisture balance in line with your natural oils and protein. If you are washing often and suffer from frizzy hair then cut back on shampoos.

If preserving your curls is your goal, apply styling products to wet or damp hair. They should elongate curls and lock in your natural curl pattern.

Ingredients that Fight Frizz

- Aloe Vera Juice
- Silicones
- Anti-Humectants

Recommendations

- Darcy's Botanicals Tucuma Butter Whip
- John Freida's Frizz Ease
- Ouidad Climate Control
- Jane Carter Incredible Curls
- Curl Junkie Curls in a Bottle

Shrinkage

It's necessary to first explain that shrinkage on natural hair speaks to its elasticity which is the hair's strength. It's actually a good sign of healthy hair to have shrinkage but I realize it does nothing for hang time.

As far as products are concerned, be sure to have the right expectations. The only job a product can do for shrinkage is to fight the humidity that causes shrinkage. You will get the real benefits from picking the right products as well as employing the right manipulation techniques.

Tips

- For type 4 hair set braid/twist styles on slightly damp to mostly dry hair
- Apply products from scalp to tip and brush or comb through to spread
- Gels with emollients soften and elongate curls by weighing them down (butters do too)

Ingredients that Matter for Shrinkage

- Glycerin
- Aloe Vera Gel
- Humectants

- Emollients

Recommendations

- EcoStyler Gel with oils
- Kinky Curly Custard
- Miss Jessie's Curly Pudding
- Karen's Body Beautiful Butter Love
- Bee Mine Bee Hold Curly Butter

Summary

You will win once you've discovered more about your natural hair and how to choose the right products. I know that you have a certain way you want to look and that your appearance is extremely important. Choosing to wear your hair natural is not a mistake and you can feel good knowing that once you've mastered the information in this book, you will ROCK whatever style you want. Hair care has always been important to me which is why I started my natural hair group, the Naturalistas in Nap and why I've organized over 30 events and workshops in just a few years. I know exactly how frustrating it can be when you can't wear your hair out because you don't think it looks right.

All it takes to save money choosing the right products is a few things. Know your hair, what it wants and how to treat it well. Understand hair products, what they do and how to test them.

Lastly, figure out which products and ingredients are good for your hair. Avoid the common advice and learn how to discern for yourself how best to treat your hair. I promise you'll feel so free once you get to that place.

Update April 2015

You have inspired me so much since I published the original copy of this book last year. You feed me with your questions, your comments and observations and the moments when you come to peace with your hair. Be sure to save my email and connect with me at info@daricerene.com. I look forward to hearing from you.

What's next?

Expect to take time putting this information to use. We've already learned how to get by and so we've developed certain habits. I would expect that the next time you step into a beauty aisle after reading this book that you're going to be a bit more curious and a bit more analytical than you were before. You're going to pick up bottles, turn them around and think about what you've read here. That's great. You are a better consumer and smarter with your money. Keep in mind that you have work to do. Buy what you think will work based on the claims, the ingredient list and what you know about your hair. Take your product home and test it. Over time, I'm positive that those trips to the beauty aisle are going to take less time because you'll walk in the store in Power Mode! That's when you've figured out your Gold Star Ingredients and your Natural Hair Profile™ and you can put it ALL to work.

I'd love to hear about your progress and keep up with your journey. My home on the web is www.thewaytonaturalhair.com and I love social media so feel free to Tweet Me @daricerene or find me on Instagram @daricerene or LinkedIn @daricerene. I'd love to keep you updated as I add more eBooks, eCourses, Webinars and events so sign up for my newsletter at www.naturalhairindy.com. Stay in touch. #PleaseandThankYou

Thank You!

Anytime you step out into the unknown it's uncomfortable. Writing this book has been a necessary challenge for me so I am grateful to you for reading it. My hope is that you will learn something valuable that will help you on your natural hair journey.

If you've enjoyed this book, I'd love it if you would leave a review. It would help me to continue to reach more people and share this information. It will only take a minute to rate the book on Amazon.

Thank you in advance for your help.